SEED CATALOGUE

Robert Kroetsch has had a tremendous influence on recent directions in Canadian writing and publishing. He was born in 1927 in Heisler, Alberta. At present he resides in Winnipeg and teaches at the University of Manitoba. His novels include *The Studhorse Man*, for which he won the Governor General's Award for Fiction in 1969, *Badlands, What the Crow Said*, and *Alibi. The Ledger, Field Notes, Advice to My Friends* and *Excerpts from the Real World* are among his numerous books of poetry. Robert Kroetsch recently received the Killam Award and was named a Fellow of the Royal Society of Canada. He is now writing a study of narrative in Canada.

Seed Catalogue

Robert Kroetsch

Turnstone Press

Turnstone Press
607-100 Arthur Street
Artspace Building
Winnipeg, MB
R3B 1H3 Canada
www.TurnstonePress.com

Turnstone Press gratefully acknowledges the assistance of The Canada
Council for the Arts, the Manitoba Arts Council, the Government of
Canada through the Book Publishing Industry Development Program
and the Government of Manitoba through the Department of Culture,
Heritage and Tourism, Arts Branch for our publishing activities.

This issue of "Seed Catalogue" is partially reprinted from earlier edi-
tions. "Seed Catalogue" is from *FIELD NOTES: The Collected Poetry of
Robert Kroetsch*. Reprinted by permission of General Publishing Co.
Limited, Toronto, Canada.

  Canadä

Cover design: Steven Rosenberg

This book was typeset by Communigraphics and printed by
Friesens for Turnstone Press

Printed in Canada
Seventh printing: September, 2010

National Library of Canada Cataloguing in Publication Data

Kroetsch, Robert, 1927-
  Seed catalogue
  Poems.
  ISBN 0-88801-109-1

I. Title
PS8521.R72S32   1986   C811'.54   C86-099048-0
PR9199.3.K76S32 1986

"Seed Catalogue" is part of a lifelong poem; the most recent volume is *Excerpts from the Real World* (Oolichan, 1986). "Spending the Morning on the Beach" is the most recently completed section of the ongoing poem. It is part of volume three of *Field Notes*, a volume to be called *Country & Western*.

for Dave & Dennis

Contents

I

Seed Catalogue

1.

No. 176—Copenhagen Market Cabbage: "This new
introduction, strictly speaking, is in every respect a
thoroughbred, a cabbage of highest pedigree, and is creating
considerable flurry among professional gardeners all over
the world."

We took the storm windows/off
the south side of the house
and put them on the hotbed.
Then it was spring. Or, no:
then winter was ending.

> "I wish to say we had lovely success
> this summer with the seed purchased
> of you. We had the finest Sweet
> Corn in the country, and Cabbage
> were dandy."
> —W.W. Lyon, South Junction, Man.

> My mother said:
> Did you wash your ears?
> You could grow cabbages
> in those ears.

Winter was ending.
This is what happened:
we were harrowing the garden.
You've got to understand this:
I was sitting on the horse.
The horse was standing still.
I fell off.

The hired man laughed: how
in hell did you manage to
fall off a horse that was
standing still?

Bring me the radish seeds,
my mother whispered.

Into the dark of January
the seed catalogue bloomed

a winter proposition, if
spring should come, then,

with illustrations:

No. 25—**McKenzie's Improved Golden Wax Bean**: "THE
MOST PRIZED OF ALL BEANS. **Virtue** is its **own reward.**
We have had **many expressions** from **keen discriminating
gardeners extolling our seed** and **this variety.**"

Beans, beans,
the musical fruit;
the more you eat,
the more you virtue.

My mother was marking the first row
with a piece of binder twine, stretched
between two pegs.

The hired man laughed: just
about planted the little bugger.
Cover him up and see what grows.

My father didn't laugh. He was puzzled
by any garden that was smaller than a
¼-section of wheat and summerfallow.

the home place: N.E. 17-42-16-W4th Meridian.

the home place: 1½ miles west of Heisler, Alberta,
                on the correction line road
                and 3 miles south.

No trees
around the house.
Only the wind.
Only the January snow.
Only the summer sun.
The home place:
a terrible symmetry.

How do you grow a gardener?

                    Telephone Peas
                    Garden Gem Carrots
                    Early Snowcap Cauliflower
                    Perfection Globe Onions
                    Hubbard Squash
                    Early Ohio Potatoes

This is what happened—at my mother's wake. This
is a fact—the World Series was in progress. The
Cincinnati Reds were playing the Detroit Tigers.
It was raining. The road to the graveyard was barely
passable. The horse was standing still. Bring me
the radish seeds, my mother whispered.

2.

My father was mad at the badger: the badger was digging holes in the potato patch, threatening man and beast with broken limbs (I quote). My father took the double-barrelled shotgun out into the potato patch and waited.

Every time the badger stood up, it looked like a little man, come out of the ground. Why, my father asked himself—Why would so fine a fellow live under the ground? Just for the cool of roots? The solace of dark tunnels? The blood of gophers?

My father couldn't shoot the badger. He uncocked the shotgun, came back to the house in time for breakfast. The badger dug another hole. My father got mad again. They carried on like that all summer.

> *Love is an amplification*
> *by doing/ over and over.*
>
> *Love is a standing up*
> *to the loaded gun.*
>
> *Love is a burrowing.*

One morning my father actually shot at the badger. He killed a magpie that was pecking away at a horse turd about fifty feet beyond and to the right of the spot where the badger had been standing.

A week later my father told the story again. In that version he intended to hit the magpie. Magpies, he explained, are a nuisance. They eat robins' eggs. They're harder to kill than snakes, jumping around the way they do, nothing but feathers.

Just call me sure-shot,
my father added.

3.

No. 1248—**Hubbard Squash:** "As **mankind** seems to have a **particular fondness** for squash, **Nature** appears to have **especially** provided this **matchless** variety of **superlative flavor.**"

> *Love is a leaping up
> and down.*
>
> *Love
> is a beak in the warm flesh.*

"As a cooker, it heads the list for warted squash. The vines are of strong running growth; the fruits are large, olive shaped, of a deep rich green color, the rind is smooth..."

But how do you grow a lover?

This is the God's own truth:
playing dirty is a mortal sin
the priest told us, you'll go to hell
and burn forever (with illustrations) —

it was our second day of catechism
—Germaine and I went home that
afternoon   if it's that bad, we
said to each other   we realized
we better quit   we realized

let's do it just one last time
and quit.

This is the God's own truth:
catechism, they called it,
the boys had to sit in the pews
on the right, the girls on the left.
Souls were like underwear that you
wore inside. If boys and girls sat
together —

Adam and Eve got caught
playing dirty.

This is the truth.
We climbed up into a granary
full of wheat   to the gunny sacks
the binder twine was shipped in —

we spread the paper from the sacks
smooth sheets   on the soft wheat
Germaine and I   we were like/one

we had discovered, don't ask me
how, where—but when the priest said
playing dirty we knew — well —

he had named it   he had named
our world   out of existence
(the horse   was standing still)

—This is my first confession. Bless me father I played
   dirty so long, just the other day, up in the granary
   there by the car shed—up there on the Brantford Binder
   Twine gunny sacks and the sheets of paper—Germaine
   with her dress up and her bloomers down —

—Son. For penance, keep your peter in your pants
for the next thirteen years.

But how —

> Adam and Eve and Pinch-Me
> went down to the river to swim—
> Adam and Eve got drownded.

But how do you grow a lover?

> We decided we could do it
> just one last time.

4.

It arrived in winter, the seed catalogue, on a January
day. It came into town on the afternoon train.

Mary Hauck, when she came west from Bruce County,
Ontario, arrived in town on a January day. She brought
along her hope chest.

She was cooking in the Heisler Hotel. The Heisler Hotel
burned down on the night of June 21, 1919. Everything
in between: lost. Everything: an absence

of satin sheets
of embroidered pillow cases
of tea towels and English china
of silver serving spoons.

How do you grow a prairie town?

> The gopher was the model.
> Stand up straight:
> telephone poles
> grain elevators
> church steeples.
> Vanish, suddenly: the
> gopher was the model.

How do you grow a past/
to live in

the absence of silkworms

the absence of clay and wattles (whatever the hell
they are)

the absence of Lord Nelson

the absence of kings and queens

the absence of a bottle opener, and me with a vicious
attack of the 26-ounce flu

the absence of both Sartre and Heidegger

the absence of pyramids

the absence of lions

the absence of lutes, violas and xylophones

the absence of a condom dispenser in the Lethbridge Hotel,
and me about to screw an old Blood whore.
I was in love.

the absence of the Parthenon, not to mention the Cathé-
drale de Chartres

the absence of psychiatrists

the absence of sailing ships

the absence of books, journals, daily newspapers and every-
thing else but the *Free Press Prairie Farmer*
and *The Western Producer*

the absence of gallows (with apologies to Louis Riel)

the absence of goldsmiths

the absence of the girl who said that if the Edmonton
Eskimos won the Grey Cup she'd let me kiss her
nipples in the foyer of the Palliser Hotel. I don't
know where she got to.

the absence of Heraclitus

the absence of the Seine, the Rhine, the Danube, the Tiber
and the Thames. Shit, the Battle River ran dry
one fall. The Strauss boy could piss across it. He
could piss higher on a barn wall than any of us.
He could piss right clean over the principal's
new car.

the absence of ballet and opera
the absence of Aeneas

How do you grow a prairie town?

Rebuild the hotel when it burns down. Bigger. Fill it
full of a lot of A-1 Hard Northern bullshitters.

—You ever hear the one about the woman who buried
her husband with his ass sticking out of the ground
so that every time she happened to walk by she could
give it a swift kick?

—Yeh, I heard it.

5.

I planted some melons, just to see what would
happen. Gophers ate everything.

> I applied to the Government.
> I wanted to become a postman,
> to deliver real words
> to real people.
>
> There was no one to receive
> my application.

I don't give a damn if I do die do die do die do die do die
do die do die do die do die do die do die do die do die do
die do die do die do die do die do die do die do die do die
do

6.

No. 339—McKenzie's Pedigreed Early Snowcap Cauli-
flower: "Of the many varieties of vegetables in existence,
Cauliflower is unquestionably one of the greatest inheri-
tances of the present generation, particularly Western
Canadians. There is no place in the world where better
cauliflowers can be grown than right here in the West. The
finest specimens we have ever seen, larger and of better
quality, are annually grown here on our prairies. Being
particularly a high altitude plant it thrives to a point of per-
fection here, seldom seen in warmer climes."

But how do you grow a poet?

Start: with an invocation
invoke—

His muse is
his muse/if
memory is

and you have
no memory then
no meditation
no song (shit
we're up against it)

how about that girl
you felt up in the
school barn or that
girl you necked with
out by Hastings' slough
and ran out of gas with
and nearly froze to
death with/ or that
girl in the skating
rink shack who had on
so much underwear you
didn't have enough
prick to get past her/
CCM skates

Once upon a time in the village of Heisler—

—Hey, wait a minute.
   That's a story.

How do you grow a poet?

For appetite: cod-liver
oil.
For bronchitis: mustard
plasters.
For pallor and failure to fill
the woodbox: sulphur
& molasses.
For self-abuse: ten Our
Fathers & ten Hail Marys.
For regular bowels: Sunny Boy
Cereal.

How do you grow a poet?

"It's a pleasure to advise that I
won the First Prize at the Calgary
Horticultural Show...This is my
first attempt. I used your seeds."

> Son, this is a crowbar.
> This is a willow fencepost.
> This is a sledge.
> This is a roll of barbed wire.
> This is a bag of staples.
> This is a claw hammer.

We give form to this land by running
a series of posts and three strands
of barbed wire around a ¼-section.

> First off I want you to take that
> crowbar and drive 1,156 holes
> in that gumbo.
> And the next time you want to
> write a poem
> we'll start the haying.

How do you grow a poet?

> This is a prairie road.
> This road is the shortest distance
> between nowhere and nowhere.
> This road is a poem.

17

Just two miles up the road
you'll find a porcupine
dead in the ditch. It was
trying to cross the road.

As for the poet himself
we can find no record
of his having traversed
the land/in either direction

no trace of his coming
or going/only a scarred
page, a spoor of wording
a reduction to mere black

and white/a pile of rabbit
turds that tells us
all spring long
where the track was

poet...say uncle.

How?

Rudy Wiebe: "You must lay great black steel lines of
fiction, break up that space with huge design and, like
the fiction of the Russian steppes, build a giant
artifact. No song can do that..."

February 14, 1976. Rudy, you
took us there: to the Oldman River
Lorna & Byrna, Ralph & Steve and me
you showed us where
the Bloods surprised the Crees
in the next coulee/ surprised
them to death. And after
you showed us Rilke's word
Lebensgliedes.

Rudy: Nature thou art.

7.

Brome Grass (Bromus Inermis): "No amount of cold will kill it. It **withstands** the summer suns. Water may stand on it for several weeks without apparent injury. The roots push through the soil, throwing up new plants continually. It **starts quicker** than other grasses in the spring. **Remains green** longer in the fall. **Flourishes under absolute neglect.**

The end of winter:
seeding/time.

*How do you grow
a poet?*

(a)

I was drinking with Al Purdy. We went round and round
in the restaurant on top of the Chateau Lacombe. We
were the turning center in the still world, the winter
of Edmonton was hardly enough to cool our out-sights.

The waitress asked us to leave. She was rather insistent;
we were bad for business, shouting poems at the paying
customers. Twice, Purdy galloped a Cariboo horse
right straight through the dining area.

Now that's what I call
a piss-up.

"No song can do that."

(b)

No. 2362—**Imperialis Morning
Glory**: "This is the wonderful
Japanese Morning Glory, cele-
brated the world over for its
wondrous beauty of both flow-
ers and foliage."

Sunday, January 12, 1975. This evening after
rereading *The Double Hook*: looking at Japanese prints.
Not at actors. Not at courtesans. Rather: Hiroshige's
series, *Fifty-Three Stations on the Tokaido.*

From the *Tokaido* series: "Shono-Haku-u." The
bare-assed travellers, caught in a sudden shower.
Men and trees, bending. How it is in a rain shower/
that you didn't see coming. And couldn't have avoided/
even if you had.

> The double hook:
> the home place.
>
> The stations of the way:
> the other garden
>
> *Flourishes.*
> *Under absolute neglect.*

(c)

Jim Bacque said (I was waiting for a plane,
after a reading; Terminal 2, Toronto)—he said,
You've got to deliver the pain to some woman,
don't you?

—Hey, Lady.
    You at the end of the bar.
    I wanna tell you something.

—Yuh?

—Pete Knight—of Crossfield,
    Alberta. Bronc-Busting Champion
    of the World. You ever hear of
    Pete Knight, the King of All
    Cowboys, Bronc-Busting Champion
    of the World?

—Huh-uh.

—You know what I mean? King
    of *All* Cowboys...Got
    killed—by a horse.
    He fell off.

—You some kind of a nut
    or something?

8.

> We silence words
> by writing them down.

THIS IS THE LAST WILL AND TESTAMENT
OF ME, HENRY L. KROETSCH:

(a) [yes, his first bequest]

To my son Frederick my carpenter tools.

It was his first bequest. First,
a man must build.

Those horse-barns around Heisler—
those perfectly designed barns
with the rounded roofs—only Freddie
knew how to build them. He mapped
the parklands with perfect horse-barns.

> I remember my Uncle Freddie.
> (The farmers no longer
> use horses.)
>
> Back in the 30s, I remember
> he didn't have enough money
> to buy a pound of coffee.
>
> Every morning at breakfast
> he drank a cup of hot water
> with cream and sugar in it.

Why, I asked him one morning—
I wasn't all that old—why
do you do that? I asked him.

Jesus Christ, he said. He was
a gentle man, really. Don't you
understand *anything?*

9.

The danger of merely living.

a shell/exploding
in the black sky: a
strange planting

a bomb/exploding
in the earth: a
strange

man/falling
on the city.
Killed him dead.

It was a strange
planting.

the absence of my cousin who was shot down while bombing
the city that was his maternal great-grandmother's
birthplace. He was the navigator. He guided himself
to that fatal occasion:

> —a city he had
> forgotten
> —a woman he had
> forgotten

He intended merely to release a cargo of bombs on a
target and depart. The exploding shell was:

a) an intrusion on a design that was not his, or

b) an occurrence which he had in fact, unintentionally, himself designed, or

c) it is essential that we understand this matter because:

He was the first descendant of that family to return to the Old Country. He took with him: a cargo of bombs.

Anna Weller: *Geboren* Cologne, 1849.
Kenneth MacDonald: Died Cologne, 1943.

A terrible symmetry.

A strange muse: forgetfulness. Feeding her far children to ancestral guns, blasting them out of the sky, smack/ into the earth. Oh, she was the mothering sort. Blood/ on her green thumb.

10.

After the bomb/blossoms   *Poet, teach us*
After the city/falls   *to love our dying.*
After the rider/falls
(the horse   *West is a winter place.*
standing still)   *The palimpsest of prairie*

under the quick erasure
of snow, invites a flight.

How/do you grow a garden?

(a)

No. 3060—**Spencer Sweet Pea:**
Pkt. 10¢; oz. 25¢;
¼ lb. 75¢; ½ lb. $1.25.

Your sweet peas
climbing the staked
chicken wire,
climbing the stretched
binder twine by
the front porch

taught me the smell
of morning, the grace
of your tired
hands, the strength
of a noon sun, the
color of prairie grass

taught me the smell
of my sweating armpits.

(b)

How do you a garden grow?
How do you grow a garden?

"Dear Sir,

The longest brome grass I remember seeing was
one night in Brooks. We were on our way up to the Calgary
Stampede, and reached Brooks about 11 pm, perhaps earlier
because there was still a movie on the drive-in screen.
We unloaded Cindy, and I remember tying her up to the truck
box and the brome grass was up to her hips. We laid down
in the back of the truck—on some grass I pulled by hand—
and slept for about three hours, then drove into Calgary.

Amie"

(c)

No trees
around the house,
only the wind.
Only the January snow.
Only the summer sun.

Adam and Eve got drownded—
Who was left?

II

Spending the Morning
on the Beach

ten related lyrics

"We all live in the same world's sea. We cannot tell a story that leaves us outside, and when I say we, I include you. But in order to include you, I feel that I cannot spend these pages saying *I* to a second person. Therefore let us say *he*, and stand together looking at them."

George Bowering, *Burning Water*

I can no longer keep a journal. My life erases everything I write.

Fiji

Realizing the poem for him has lost its expectancy, he
heads directly for Fiji. He flies by Air New Zealand, out
of L.A. Nadi is dark to his landing.

The Southern Cross signals the upset world. Even
westward is lost in east. We are not where we were.

This island's murder was for sandalwood. The European
trader and the Chinese aesthete drank tea together
without shame. Any aesthetic has a terrible will. He
registers at The Sandalwood Inn.

Waiting for the dining room to open, he hikes down to
the beach. The parrots in the coconut palms are noisy in
the sunrise.

Somewhere in his recent flying is a lost day. Words are
like that. Once upon a time he was a gardener of the
possible fruition.

Here in Fiji he drinks the juice of passion fruit, he eats
papaya and a thin slice of fresh pineapple for breakfast.

Brisbane

There is salt on his skin.

Realizing he's no longer obliged by the ache in his body to write poems, he watches the grasstrees burning free of their dead leaves. The squat black trunks exhaling wisps of smoke wear each and fashionably a tassle of green hair. All this, just as he'd begun to hope for a vision of hell. At lunch, for instance, he's joined by a pair of kookaburras, hopping down from a gum tree onto the balcony of the Griffith University Club. We come to conclusions. He calls to mind Odysseus, somewhere on a beach, hiding his nakedness yet keeping it available. The skinks loll in the sun, the possum sleeps toward an awakening of darkness.

There is salt in the fluids of his body.

He has the whole day.

Noosa Heads 1

On the way up to Noosa Heads he stops in a cloud of gum
trees to visit an avocado farm. The avocado trees, in eight
varieties, drip avocados into a sequence of harvest times.
He breaks in two a custard apple. The seeds are covered in
a white substance that is almost slimy, yet sweet to the
tongue. He climbs a road to a banana plantation, the fruit
growing ripe in blue plastic bags high on the tall plants.
After fruiting the plant dies.

He goes with Doug into Noosa National Park. They are
two poets on vacation. But what do poets take vacations
from? What, ever, is the possibility of other? They hike
into the native forest. They find the nude beach,
Alexandria, and take off their clothes and lie on the sand.

Realizing the poem is the tormentor of his sleep, he
strangles it by his refusal, in the hot sunlight, to close his
eyes. Each surfer is a small miracle of stillness and motion.
Each surfer slips down a rising wave, then disappears into
a bed of foam.

Doug tries bodysurfing. He engages the windmill of his
own recklessness. The sun recovers him.

Noosa Heads 2

20 May 86
sunrise 6:23
sunset 5:05

Realizing *poetry* is a mousetrap on the tongue, he calls ashore for water.

He is somewhere under the failed wave. The sand scours his eyes. He hardly bothers to hold his breath.

The self-portrait is a found object, signed by yours truly, as we all know. Climbing the dunes behind the beach, he finds the shade of a tree.

It is Doug, alone on the beach, who learns the semiotics of nakedness. It's a matter of spacing, Doug says.

It's a matter of knowing when to look and when not to look.

The mathematics of the gaze: angle and tangent and the theory of the line.

The self-portrait is a found object, given a name by another, appropriated. The slide (the sly) of metonymy.

It is early winter, a morning in May.

Geelong, Victoria

Realizing the poem. Talking the poem onto the page or writing the poem onto the tongue. Realizing he cannot foil his own inertia, he steals a pomegranate.

The fruit in Brian's garden: fig, lemon, peach, pomegranate, pear, apricot, lime, apple, kiwi, passion fruit and feijoa. Not atoll, says the cockatoo.

Brian foretells the future by riding a surfboard along the edge of a hurricane. Even now, the Solomon Islands lie in devastation.

At the waterfront they find a fishing boat unloading its morning catch. A Vietnamese man and woman, elderly, are dickering for snapper. One of the fishermen rinses two fish over the side of the boat, then fillets them on the deck.

Dropping the bones back into the water.

Spitting out the seeds, into the water, is half the fun.

Sydney

Realizing that light, not dark, is the poet's affliction, he gives himself the Governor General's Award For Not Writing Poetry for the year 1999.

He leaves his hotel in Kings Cross and goes to see the art show, ORIGINS ORIGINALITY + BEYOND, The Biennale of Sydney 1986.

He stops first at The Art Gallery of New South Wales, then buys a map and finds his way to Pier 2/3, on Walsh Bay, where the larger works are on display in an old pier building.

Magdalena Abakanowicz, SEVEN STANDING FIGURES
Robert Adrian, 76 AIRPLANES
Julie Brown-Rrap, BREAK AND ENTER—EXHIBITS 1-4

Braco Dimitrijević, MEMORIES OF COLUMBUS' FRIEND
Richard Killeen, TIME TO CHANGE THE GREEK HERO
 Wolfgang Laib, THE SIXTY-THREE RICE MEALS FOR A STONE

Vivienne Shark Lewitt, LAST NIGHT I DREAMED I WENT TO
                                            MANDALAY AGAIN
Rainer Mang, DEUTSCHER MANN SUCHT WAS
Carlo Maria Mariani, GUARDASI IN UNO SPECCHIO CELESTE
                (LOOKING AT ONESELF IN A HEAVENLY MIRROR)

Marta Minujin, THE BOOK'S PARTHENON
Luigi Ontani, YOUNG MAN WITH FRUITS
Therese Oulton, MORTAL COIL

Yumiko Sugano, WHALE'S GENERATION
Masami Teraoka, HANAUMA BAY SERIES/CAMERA CREW
                                        AND BLOWHOLE 1
Michael Nelson Tjakamarra, POSSUM DREAMING

Anon, Canada, 1927, SELF-PORTRAIT OF POET or
                        THROWING IN THE TOWEL, EH?

Wellington, New Zealand

Realizing he is done with poetry, he goes to a museum to
see a reconstruction of an extinct New Zealand bird, a bird
that was flightless, huge, possibly the largest bird (height
to 12 feet) that ever lived, the Giant Moa. Now how's that
for self-pity?

The poem as quotation:

> Merino Sheep: The oldest and most numerous breed
> in the world. Originated in Spain or North Africa.
> First sheep in NZ. Captain Cook brought four in
> 1773, they did not survive. Wool: fine fibre, used in
> quality woollen and worsted fabrics.
>
> Feel free to stroke Lindale's stock through the fence.
>
> Murray Grey Cattle: This breed came about by
> accident when in 1902 a Shorthorn cow was crossed
> with a black Angus bull, the result a grey calf, a
> Mulberry. This unwanted cow survived to produce 12
> Mulberries. The name change came in the 1960s. Very
> adaptable, the breed has prospered in NZ conditions
>
> Sheep and cattle may nibble for nuts but will not bite.

The poem as evasion.
The poem as resignation.
The poem as a net
that drowns fish.
The poem as a postcard
sent directly to the sun.
The poem as POET TREE.

Rotorua

Realizing that poetry is a hospital for the sane, he watches the Maoris building their replica village.

The thermal reserve, Whakarewarewa. A volcano's dream of a poem. Pohutu Geyser, as unpredictable as love. The mud pools bubble and pop, under the twisting steam. The forest tries to untie itself.

He cannot take the light in his hands. Pumice and sulphur. If the volcano's crater becomes a lake. If the beach itself is beached, high and dry.

Orpheus, nothing, says the parakeet.

Orifice.

If the carved boat floats in a sheltered pool, and the iconic face bites its defiant tongue, then we have come to see the picture.

North of Auckland, Parry Kauri Park

They are in the park. The sign at the gate says the park
will be locked at 5 pm. It is 5:05. The park is locked.

The larger of the two kauri trees is eight centuries old.
The second tree, only 25 feet in girth, is younger by two
centuries. The flock of rosellas inhabits the crown of the
older tree.

Or are those birds, more exactly, red-crowned parakeets?
He lifts the lenses of his glasses against the drift of rain.
The rain lifts the coastline into these hills.

He and Steve climb out of the half-ton just as the old
woman appears from her cottage door, makes a smart
right turn, begins her approach.

(It was earlier in the morning. The paddock was all steep
hillside. Steve ordered the dog to bring in the cattle. The
dog in one easy leap cleared the high fence.)

You didn't read the sign, did you? the old woman says, at
once patient and yet a bit testy.

It looks that way, he tells her. I realize that.

The Hibiscus Coast

Realizing the poem is a cruising shark, he curls his toes in
the mud.

The horses train softly on the hard sand. He drops his
camera into a mangrove swamp. He believes it was an
accident. The man in the shed by the mangroves is
building a boat.

There are sharks in these waters, the Maori farmer says,
but not so many as on land. His wife goes into the
paddock to feed her horses and latches the gate.

Hibiscus. Herbs, shrubs or small trees of the mallow
family. With dentate leaves and large showy flowers. They
grow around the gas stations, even. And in the parking
lots.

Sighting two dolphins, just out from shore, rising and
gracefully diving, he hurries into the water.

Recent Publications from Turnstone Press

People of the Interlake by Andrew Blicq & Ken Gigliotti

Bloody Jack by Dennis Cooley

The Magic Trumpet by Victor Cowie & Victor Davies

Surviving the Paraphrase by Frank Davey

Grasshopper by Helen Hawley

Mister Spock, Do You Read Me? by Mary Horodyski

Thin Poems by James Hutchison

Backing into Heaven by Steve Noyes

i sing for my dead in german by Audrey Poetker

The Best Possible Face: L.B. Foote's Winnipeg by Douglas Smith & Michael Olito

No Fixed Admission by Jacqui Smyth

Headframe: by Birk Sproxton

Trace: Prairie Writers on Writing. Ed. Birk Sproxton

The Cartier Street Contract by Wayne Tefs

Waiting for Saskatchewan by Fred Wah

After the Revolution by John Weier